LET ME BE

MAUREEN ANNE MEEHAN

LET ME BE

Copyright © 2024 by Maureen Anne Meehan

ISBN: 979-8-3303-1788-2

www. maureenmeehanbooks.com
info@maureenmeehan.com

Table of Contents

LET ME BE DEDICATION

Let Me Be is dedicated to all readers who are searching for the needle in the haystack of the utter hell of dating on dating apps littered with liars' cheaters and ne'er-do-wells of the dating world. It is a tricky mind field out there and it is very easy to detonate bombs.

To these faithful ones who are honest and trustworthy: guard your good qualities and be patient, for there are some good folks out there looking for love. They are difficult to find. But they exist. I hope.

May your troubles be less and your blessings be more. And nothing but happiness comes through your door. To all the days here and after, may they be filled with fond memories, happiness, and laughter.

Chapter 1

Let me Go

Let Me Go

Let me be free, Stop keeping restraints on me. You haven't walked in my shoes, I hope you never do. Do you have the love of your life? I hope you always do. I have been injured and maimed. I have wanted to die to want to live again. I've never wanted anything like I want to love again right now. Leave me alone to let me find love. You have been as lucky as I was once. I am not a poet but I am a writer. I wish I were a poet because maybe I would have a lover. Hemingway had so many ideas to write about. Love? Yes. He had it all. But he was lonely. He never understood and the difference is that I do understand. Leave me alone.

She was dating a new man and her daughter felt like things were moving too fast. Her daughter expressed her concern about the rush to move forward at such a breakneck pace. The mother tried to explain that she had been alone and lonely for a very long time and that she was ready to find love again. The daughter understood that but could not get her head around the pacing issue.

After due consideration of the conversation with her daughter, she decided that her daughter was right. The pacing was off. Too fast. Almost desperate. Her analysis led her to the conclusion that she was trying to fit a square peg in a round hole due to loneliness. She realized that her motivation was misdirected and that she should re-think the pacing and possibly the subject of her affections. She was settling just out of loneliness.

It dawned on her that she had raised a smart cookie in a

daughter. She had set good examples and had raised her daughter to be open and honest about her feelings. That was a good thing. The mom had to talk with her daughter and acknowledge her daughter's maturity and courage to broach the sensitive subject.

Over time, the mother realized that the square peg round hole situation would never work. Too many red flags. The mother explained this to her

wise daughter and they agreed that maybe it was a good strategy to slow down and look at the quality of the man. Not only to what they had in common but to also consider what they did not have in common. One of those things was that this man had not been a very good father. His children were "failures to launch" and were not setting or accomplishing goals. That's a parenting issue. Another red flag was self-confidence. Mom had plenty. He was obviously lacking to some extent. She caught him snooping on her phone. This act not only shows a lack of Self-confidence, but self-control and respect for privacy.

Ultimately the mother cut ties with the square peg and it was clearly for the best. Wise daughter!

Chapter 2

SHE IS NOT THE ONE

SHE IS NOT THE ONE

Pay now or pay later is how the old adage goes and this applies to work, parenting, love, and other aspects of life. Paying later is generally more costly and taxing. If she's not the one now, she won't be the one later. Call it. Cut the cord. Move on.

He had been dating her for over a year and she had recently moved in with him. Things were going well at first, but over time he realized that the dynamics of the relationship had changed since they started living together.

She was becoming clingy and demanding of his time and he did not appreciate it. He had a lot of hobbies and interests and friends that he enjoyed spending time with. She seemed not to have nearly as many hobbies or friends. And she had a nosey controlling mother. That was becoming more and more of an issue.

He went golfing with a friend to discuss how he was feeling and his buddy finally had the courage to tell him that he did not care for her for a number of reasons including clinginess. He appreciated his friend's honesty as he knew that once a friend announces a dislike of a companion, there is no turning back.

He then went out for a drink with his father to discuss his feelings and his father listened intently before commenting. Once the son was finished explaining his growing concerns, the father wisely explained that if the son was having these feelings in the early stages of a relationship these feelings would likely intensify over time and build resentment. The father wisely advised that it would be best to extricate from this relationship earlier rather than later because if he went forward with what the girlfriend wanted, which was marriage, the marriage would likely not last and a divorce is one thing – but a divorce involving children is a whole other animal.

The son took this sage advice to heart and asked to speak with his girlfriend. He explained how he was feeling and that he had decided to call it off and ask her to move out. He felt terrible for hurting her feelings so deeply, but ultimately it was how he felt and he didn't want to delay this any longer.

She was extremely upset over the breakup which of course he knew was a natural behavior. But her tears did not dissuade him. He offered to rent her some type of temporary accommodation for her to get on her feet again. He was a gentleman after all. She declined the offer and moved out. It was not a good breakup, but are they ever good?

Chapter 3

HE'S NOT YOUR BABY DADDY

HE'S NOT YOUR BABY DADDY

She is the mother of two young children and the father of the children flew the coop when she announced that she was pregnant again.

She had no support from her father and she needed to either take on a second job to support these babies or she was going to need to find a man to help her support and raise her children. This is easier said than done.

She had been dating a man for a few months and he told her that he didn't mind if she had children.

She decided to test the water and invite him over for dinner one Saturday because she no longer could afford a babysitter and she had run out of favors from her friends.

He agreed to go to her apartment for dinner and arrived timely with a bottle of wine and some flowers.

The kids were sitting in front of the television watching a show and were shy about meeting him at first. He didn't seem overwhelmingly engaged with the children and gave up fairly easily on trying to engage them. He easily could have asked them what they were watching or otherwise engaged with them but he wanted attention from her.

She opened the wine poured them each a glass and put the flowers in a vase of water. They sat on the couch near the children and shared wine and conversation while the children watched their show. When it was time for dinner, she paused the movie and got the kids situated at the dinner table. She was working on plating the food and not only did he not offer to help her, he did not sit at the dinner table and try once again to talk with the kids. She noticed.

During dinner, the kids were their normal loud selves and spilled milk and made messes. They were young. This is normal. He seemed annoyed that she needed to address the children and not engage with him as much as she would have if they were out on a date without the kids.

After dinner, she resumed the show for the kids and started to clear the table and clean up. Again, he did not offer to help her, and he did not join the kids and spend time with them. He simply enjoyed his wine and talked with her – mostly about himself.

As the night wore on, it was time to get the children in the bath and get them ready for bed. This is a time-consuming part of the day. Bath time was something that the kids enjoyed and they liked to play in the tub with their toys and splash about. Once in their pajamas, it was story time before bed and she laid down with them on her bed and read them a story.
She often fell asleep herself during story time as it was her typical end of the day and she was exhausted.

He did not join them for story time and stayed in the living room watching TV. When they were tucked in she joined her boyfriend on the couch. He seemed annoyed and continued to watch his sports program instead of focusing on her.

He was expecting to spend the night, which he had done in the past after the kids were in bed, but she was simply too tired and needed to go to sleep. She took the kids to church on Sunday mornings and she needed rest. She explained this to him and told him that it was time for him to leave. He left. She never heard from him again.

Chapter 4

RELUCTANT TO WALK DOWN THE AISLE

RELUCTANT TO WALK DOWN THE AISLE

They had been dating for eight years and she had made it perfectly clear that she wanted to get married and have children before her body clock was too old. Time was ticking.

He finally popped the question with a ring but was not very creative about the proposal. She overlooked it as she was so excited to have a ring on her finger. She immediately started inquiring about where he would like to get married and when. He had no specific answers and didn't seem to want to discuss it so quickly after the engagement. She let it slide for a few weeks.

When she broached the subject of the wedding date again, he was dismissive and disinterested. This caused her concern. She talked about it with her girlfriends and her mother. His mother reminded her that they had been together for a long time and that he had not bothered to ask her father for her hand in marriage. This bothered her parents as they were old-fashioned and felt that a man should be a man about a proposal.

She gave it another month and then went out to dinner with friends, one of her girlfriends asked them whether they should "save the date" and other wedding planning details. When neither had an answer to the inquiry, her friend said that she needed to use the restroom and asked her girlfriend to join her.

In the restroom, her best friend commented on his lackluster response to her question. She explained that she didn't understand why he was hesitant to discuss the topic. Her bestie told her that she needed to be firm and direct about it as she was not getting any younger. She agreed.

When they got home from dinner she again asked to discuss the wedding planning and he rolled his eyes and told her to give it a break. He had proposed. What was the rush?

Months elapsed and he still didn't want to discuss it, so one weekend afternoon she told him that she was meeting with her best friend and her mother to look at wedding venues in the area. He didn't seem interested and he didn't want to join them. That was not a good sign.

She and her mom and bestie went to three venues and when she returned home, he was not there and didn't leave an indication as to where he had gone. Apparently, he had joined a few buddies at a local sports bar and was watching a game and drinking. He came home very late and very intoxicated.

The next morning, she made him coffee and breakfast in bed and joined him with her coffee. He was not feeling well. She began talking with him about the venues that they had visited and explained that she had found the perfect place for them to marry. He remained silent.

After his breakfast, he took a shower put on his golf clothes, and told her that he had a tee time with a buddy for the afternoon.

She was disappointed as she was hoping that he would be excited that she found a venue and she wanted him to go and visit the venue with her. He declined.

That evening when he returned from golf, she was sitting at the table having dinner alone. He grabbed some dinner and resumed watching sports in the living room. He was icing her.

She let a few days pass before asking to discuss it again. He blew a fuse. He said he wasn't ready to get married and felt like she was pestering him about it. She began to cry. She called her mom and told her what was going on. Her mom told her to call off the engagement and move out. He wasn't the One. The mother never felt that he was the One and was now in a position to tell her daughter how she and Dad felt about this young man.

She called it off and moved out and moved on, but not without sincere heartbreak.

Chapter 5

WEEKEND WARRIOR

WEEKEND WARRIOR

They met on a houseboat on Lake Havasu as they had mutual friends who were taking a week-long vacation on the river. There were jet skis and speed boats cliff jumping and all kinds of fun outdoor activities planned.

She was an avid athlete and was good at all sports. He was enamored with her ability to waterski and jet ski and swim and dive off a high cliff. He was mediocre at best at waterskiing and was afraid to jump from a cliff so high. However, he was content watching her in her bikini do her stuff.

She was toned and tan and naturally beautiful and didn't seem to notice her own beauty which made her all the more attractive to him.
As the week wore on the fun intensified as the friends got to know one another better, they played drinking games and board games at night and not only could she hold her own doing shots of tequila but she was intensely competitive at games and very smart.

As the friends were parting ways at the end of the vacation, he conjured the courage to ask for her number. She gave it to him and told him to call her.

When he got home he did call her and ask her if she wanted to go to a movie the following weekend. She said that it sounded like fun but that she already had plans with other friends to fly to Baja, Mexico for a sports fishing and surfing weekend.

He was disappointed as it seemed like she always had plans to do something extravagantly active. This pattern continued for weeks and his disappointment mounted. It wasn't that she didn't respond quickly to his texts, but she always had other plans.

Finally, he decided to ask her out midweek for dinner and a movie and that he would commute her way. She agreed and they had a great time together. She was very engaging and had so many fun stories and experiences to share. He was absolutely fascinated by her.

Again, he continued to ask her to do things on the weekends but she was always busy. She only had Tuesdays and Wednesdays available for dates. Over time, he finally garnished the courage to ask her if she was ever available on a weekend and she said that she had a boyfriend that she dated weekends only. This arrangement was not going to work out.

Chapter 6

FORE!

FORE!

He invited her to play golf at his club and offered to pick her up.

They had exchanged many photos and texts and telephone calls and she felt comfortable enough to have him drive her to the course. He arrived on time and they were off.

They checked in at the pro shop and he paid for his guest to play. He loaded the golf cart with both sets of clubs and they were off to the first tee. He hit a banger of a first shot. Hers was not great but she admitted that she hadn't played in a bit and was a little rusty.

They got through the first few holes and her game realigned. She relaxed and started to enjoy herself. He was fit for his age and a good golfer. The only thing was that he looked much older than his photos. She did notice that in every photo he sent, he had a hat on. She didn't think much about it at the time and he was wearing a hat golfing.

After golf, they had agreed to have dinner together at his club. They entered and were seated and he took off his hat. Much to her surprise, not only was he bald but he had age and liver spots on his scalp. Now he looked another 10 years older than her. She decided on the spot that this was their first and only date. She was not into bald guys with age spots on their scalp. She wished that she had driven on her own so that she could cut it short but she also didn't want to be rude.

After dinner, he drove her home carried her clubs into her garage, and put them away for her. He was a gentleman in every way. He offered to come in for a drink but she feigned a yawn and said that the heat of the day had worn her out and she needed to retire. The reality was that she was not attracted to this old-looking man.

They never saw one another again.

Chapter 7

TOO OLD FOR A BEACH WALK

TOO OLD FOR A BEACH WALK

They both lived near a local beach and agreed to meet on the sand for a sunset beach stroll before grabbing a drink at a local tavern. They both arrived around the same time in the beach parking lot. It was a casual date as it was their first. He immediately complimented her appearance and told her that she looked better than her pictures. They both agreed that it was generally their collective experience that people didn't look like their photos.

They were close in age and he claimed to be fit. He was handsome and did look like his photos but she noticed that he walked with a distinguished limp. She inquired about it asking whether he'd had a hip replacement.

He admitted that he had but said that he was still having residual pain.

He walked very slowly down the beach steps and proceeded to cruise the sand with the enthusiasm of a turtle. She liked a brisk walk and the pace was clearly not to her liking. He then asked to cut the walk short because his hip and knees were hurting. They had only been walking for 10 minutes.

They made their way to the tavern and he ordered their drinks. They sat and chatted over a cocktail while the sun was setting. They had a lot in common such as concerts and cooking and had grown up in similar households. Conversation flowed with ease and the sunset was beautiful.

However, once the sun set, it tended to cool off quickly and she used this as an excuse to cut out the date early. She never saw him again.

Chapter 8

VINO

VINO

They agreed to meet for dinner at a restaurant centrally located in between them. He chose the place and it was a nice one with great reviews. She arrived first and was seated near the window so that she could watch him walk in. He had a shopping bag with him and was wearing a nice suit with nice shoes and he had put effort into his style.

He was seated across the table from her and he retrieved two bottles of fine wine from his bag and set them on the table. The waiter opened the first to decant for them. He poured her a glass after they had ordered dinner and he noticed that she knocked it back relatively quickly. It was a very nice bottle of wine meant to be savored, not devoured, but he decided to overlook it as she might have been nervous on a first date.

He refilled her glass and once again she drained it rapidly. He kept refilling the glass out of courtesy, but they were now on the second bottle of wine and she had polished off most of the first bottle.

Dinner arrived and conversation flowed and it was an overall nice date. However, she consumed nearly two bottles of wine over the course of two hours.
He inquired about her ability to drive home and she said that she was fine.

He offered to drive her or Uber her home but she insisted on taking her own car.

She texted when she got home that she made it safely and the only thought on his mind was whether she hit any pedestrians end route.

He was not impressed and he did not offer a second date.

Chapter 9

BUILT FOR SPEED

BUILT FOR SPEED

He is the CEO of a Fortune 500 company, flies his own jet, and is into hiking, biking, cooking, and his speed boat.

He has a house on a lake in another state and he is often there for a few weeks at a time. She is an accomplished businesswoman and is polished, fit, and busy in her own corporate America. They speak several times and with busy travel schedules, they only have the following Monday available for dinner.

They agree on a nice steakhouse and meet in the bar for a drink before dinner. She arrives directly from work and is in nice business attire. He looks like he rode his Harley there dressed in biker clothes with a pot belly and a port wine spot on his cheek. He must have airbrushed this out of his photos as it was rather prominent and distracting. They shared a glass of wine and then were seated for dinner.

She ordered a steak salad and he ordered a large porterhouse rare. They each ordered a glass of cabernet with their steak.

They converse over dinner mostly about his speed boat. He speaks ad nauseum about how some guy scratched his custom-painted red boat pulling it out of the water and that it was going to cost a lot of money to repair the scratches.

It was apparently the biggest thing happening in his life

at the moment. She was bored. She ate her salad while he devoured his entire huge steak. It was a sight to witness a man eat such a large piece of protein in one sitting. No wonder he was overweight.

At the end of the night, he politely escorted her to her car and went in for the goodnight kiss. It was awful. Sloppy and underwhelming to say the very least.

She texted that she was home safe and sound and he called right away to thank her for her time and ask for a second date. She was not attracted to him at all and was appalled by his looks and eating habits. She declined a second date and he wanted to know why as he told her that he had a very nice experience.

She explained that she felt that his photos were deceptive and that he was much heavier than his photos revealed. He admitted that he was trying to lose 30 pounds. By the manner in which he consumed food, she doubted that. They did not have a second date.

Chapter 10

WASTED IN NEW YORK

WASTED IN NEW YORK

Young and in their late 20s living the dream of New York City post-college. They had a few mutual friends and they had met a few times as a group for drinks. They flirted on their last outing and had agreed to meet for their first date without mutual friends abound.

They decided to meet for drinks after work on Friday and picked a hip place where they could be alone. She was timely and dressed nicely. He was late and very, very drunk. He had gone out with friends already and had put back a few too many.

He could barely complete a sentence and she was not enjoying trying to decipher his drunk speech. She decided to cut the date short. He was everything she was looking for and checked all of the boxes, but the drunk thing was not one of them. She ordered him his own Uber and told him that they should try it again another day.

He called her a few days later to see if she wanted to meet on a Sunday late afternoon for a redo. She agreed.

He showed up again very tipsy. He'd been at a sporting event with friends earlier and had again had cocktails with his buddies. This date was not a whole lot better.

She gave up. Cheers.

Chapter 11

PILOT PROBLEMS

PILOT PROBLEMS

She met him at a bar in Burbank and they garnered conversation about career and family. He was very handsome and extremely well-educated and had a fascinating life. She was in movie production so their diversity made for fluid conversation.

He was an aerospace engineer and a flight instructor in Burbank. They were geographically desirable. But she was much busier in her career than him as he didn't instruct at night and she often worked late in the evening in post-production.

They exchanged cell phone numbers and agreed to talk and then hopefully meet for a date. And they did. Again, everything was going great. They had a great Taco Tuesday night in Burbank and truly enjoyed getting to know one another.

She asked him about his weekend plans and wanted to know if he was available to go with her to Solvang to a festival for a few days. He said that he had worked over the weekend and that his weekends were his busiest days. She understood and was going with other friends anyway.

Upon her return, they resumed conversation and she asked for his availability for the following weekend. Same response. She was available sometimes during the week but it was usually until late due to Hollywood. People started work early and worked late. Movie production looks sexy but the reality is that if you are behind the scenes, you work hard long hours.

She offered a few nights during the week and he declined with the rationale that he could not meet that late because he worked early mornings. Fair enough. Work is work.

He offered to watch a movie with her remotely and said that if they watched it in unison from their own couches, they could discuss it after the movie. It seemed weird to her since they lived only about 15 minutes away from one another but she agreed to at least try it.

They watched a movie of his choosing and to her, it was eccentric in a not-goo way. But she was a trooper and finished it with him. They spoke after and it was okay. This pattern repeated for several nights and she was bored not only with his movie selections but also the roundup discussions regarding the movies at the end of the night. This was not her idea of dating.

She finally told him that this remote dating movie night was a snore. He was upset. He thought it was going splendidly. She asked him if he did this with other women and he responded that he did. Then she asked if he was in a relationship. He said that he was married.

Chapter 12

COLLEGE KIDS

COLLEGE KIDS

They met at a fraternity party at Oklahoma State and they hit it off immediately. He was more passive and she was an outgoing sorority girl and she loved to dance. She got him out on the dance floor and things started to jive.

They dated for months and went to each other's dances and formals and football games and had a blast together. She was bringing him out of his shell.

Thanksgiving was closing in and he was going home to family, she was from out of the country and did not understand Thanksgiving and was not leaving campus so he asked her if she wanted to join him at his family home. She agreed as she watched the sorority house clear out for the holiday.

They arrive at his family home and his parents are awaiting him in the driveway. This is his first girlfriend and they are very excited to meet her and see how their son interacts with a woman.

She is very pretty and humble and nice and very intelligent and driven. She is from a country where women are not honored and for her to get an education in the United States is a big deal.

They get her settled and meet on the veranda for a glass of wine before dinner. Mom has made her son's favorite meatloaf dish with wonderful sides and more wine. They enjoy a wonderful meal and this young lady admits that she was in an orphanage most of her life and she had never been in such a beautiful home with such nice people and a home-cooked meal.

The mother was so touched by her honesty. It takes a lot to open up to one's weaknesses.

It did not go unnoticed to either Mom or her son that she had not revealed the orphanage information to him. He had no idea.

They continue to date. She is very beautiful and it is his first love. He takes her home for Christmas because her Visa does not allow her to travel. That should have been a signal.

She enjoys Christmas with this Midwest family and they fall in love with her. She loves their only son. His sisters love her. Everyone loves her. But they don't understand her abandonment issues. She needs constant attention and no one can manage it.

Time progresses and Mom asks how things are going, he's pretty stressed over her demands for his time attention, and money,

He pays for everything. She wants nice things. He is a college kid on a 529 budget.

Two years later he tells Mom and Dad everything after graduating and she has to move back to Ukraine. He was the meal ticket Visa.

Chapter 13

MOGULS WITHOUT MANNERS

MOGULS WITHOUT MANNERS

They met in the singles line skiing and ended up on the same chairlift up to the top of the mountain with plenty of time to chat.

They were both single and, in their thirties, and we both looking to meet the right person and settle down.

They lived about 30 minutes from one another in Southern California making them geographically desirable, depending on traffic. They agreed to meet up the following Sunday for dinner. He picked her up and they went to her favorite sushi bar a few blocks away. They had a wonderful meal and then proceeded to return to her house for a glass of wine.

One thing led to another and he ended up spending the night Sunday. They stayed up talking most of the night despite the fact that both of them had to work on Monday morning.

They both had busy work and social schedules so it was difficult to match calendars for the next few weekends but they managed another Sunday date. This one started mid-day and went into Monday morning once again.

She was gone the following weekend as she was visiting a girlfriend out of state and they were going to a concert. He had his own concert plans at a different venue.

She returned the following Monday and they spoke of him coming to her house for dinner Wednesday night. She went shopping on Tuesday after work and she purchased a pound of halibut to make for him with a beet salad. Wednesday morning, he texted saying that he needed to reschedule as work problems needed to be addressed. She was disappointed that he canceled but equally disappointed that he did it via text. They agreed to reschedule for Friday for dinner at her house.

Friday morning, he canceled by text again saying that his work stuff was still at issue and that he had a doctor's appointment. This was the final straw for her.

He could ski moguls but he had no manners.

Chapter 14

GYMRAT

GYM RAT

They met online and swapped out of the app after exchanging cell numbers. They spoke and used FaceTime to chat and quickly discovered that they lived only a few blocks away from one another. They agreed to meet locally for dinner on a Thursday night.

He was punctual and they agreed to take a walk on a trail overlooking the ocean before dinner. They had a great walk and talk and she learned quite a bit about him.

Dinner was a great experience with good food and service.

They decided to go back to her house after dinner and continue their date. He ended up spending the weekend with her and they truly hit it off.

They repeated this a few times with great results. They had a lot in common and they were both intelligent and articulate.

He spoke of his daughters and grandchildren and he seemed like a genuinely loving man.

One day he called her at the end of her work day and he told her that he needed to come clean about something. He told her that even though he had been separated for years from his wife, they were not final and the divorce paperwork had not been touched in years. This meant that she had been intimate with a married man and she was very upset about it. Her ethics were important to her.

What bothered her the most was that they had spent countless hours together talking and he had plenty of opportunity to tell her this tidbit. He avoided the subject instead.

They decided to not pursue the relationship.

Chapter 15

PHONE SNOOPER

PHONE SNOOPER

They met online and quickly realized that they no longer lived in the same state. He had recently retired from being a fighter pilot and a commercial pilot and he wanted to live near the mountains to ski.

Being a retired pilot meant that he could pop on a flight anytime and after a lot of communication between them, he agreed to fly out to see her and he did.

She picked him up early before she started to work and she hung out at her house while she completed her work day. They then went for a long beach walk and then returned to her house. She planned to make him an early dinner since he had such an early flight and he lived in another time zone.

She was a good cook and she made him salmon and salad. They enjoyed a nice bottle of wine together and sat in front of her fireplace and talked for hours.

They upstairs together and they had a great long weekend doing a lot of activities such as hiking, dining, spin class, etc.

She then flew to see him a few weeks later and they went skiing together for a few days. They had a great time together once again. His birthday was fast approaching and she invited him out to join her in the wine country. He agreed and flew back. They went to the wine country and enjoyed great food and wine as well as hiking, etc.

They returned to her house on a Sunday. He was supposed to fly home on Monday afternoon. She was downstairs doing laundry and when she went back upstairs, she caught his snooping through her phone.

She was shocked and surprised and asked him what he was doing. He stumbled and mumbled that he thought it was his phone. They both knew he was lying.

She told him to pack up his things and she drove him to the airport and they never saw each other again.

Chapter 16

MOTORCYCLE MADNESS

MOTORCYCLE MADNESS

They met through an online app and after some time decided to exchange numbers. One thing that they had in common was motorcycles. He still rode one and she did not. But it was an icebreaker for conversation.

She had once had a Fat Boy Harley which is a big bike for a lady and he was impressed that she was strong enough to hold it up. He used to have a Harley but now had a BMW and he loved talking about it.

So much so that in their final conversation he talked for 45 minutes straight about this motorcycle. She was bored out of her mind. She tried to change the subject several times but to no avail. She couldn't wait to hang up.

Chapter 17

PHOTO FINISH

PHOTO FINISH

They were set up on a blind date by a mutual friend and agreed to meet at a local brew house nearby for happy hour. They both were punctual upon arrival but he didn't look at all like the photos her friend had sent to her.
He was overweight and did not look like he was in good shape.
She was a fitness instructor so fitness was crucial to her.

They chatted for a bit over a drink. They mostly spoke of their respective careers. They both laughed about their dating lives and how bleak the dating apps were. Neither had had any luck with the dating apps so they were excited about a blind date set up by a friend. However, it was crystal clear to her that this was no better.

She cut it short claiming that she had work to do and the date lasted only an hour. She did take a selfie of them to show to their mutual friend.
He immediately commented on the photo something to the extent of a "cute couple". She responded that they were definitely not a couple in that he didn't look like she thought. But she did thank the mutual friend for thinking of her.

When the guy asked her out for a second date, she declined and told him that they didn't have enough in common to continue dating.

His text in response to hers was hostile. He thought that their date went well. When she didn't agree, he told her that she did not have permission to use his likeness on social media. She didn't respond, but rest assured that she had zero plans to use his photo for anything. She had already deleted it.

Chapter 18

NO LEG TO STAND ON

NO LEG TO STAND ON

They met online and agreed to meet for dinner. She arrived first and was seated at a table for two. He arrived and walked to greet her. She noticed that he walked with a slight limp.

They enjoyed a nice meal with a bottle of Bordeaux and talked for hours. When it was time to go, he walked her to her car and gave her a gentle kiss on the lips.

They agreed to have another date. This time he was granted permission to pick her up at her place. She invited him in for charcuterie and wine before dinner. They were seated on her couch and she noticed that his left leg was hanging at an odd angle. She didn't want to say anything. When they got up to leave for dinner, she watched him adjust his leg before walking.

She inquired about his leg and he told her that he was an amputee from the knee down due to a car accident in high school.

She felt poorly for him but felt like he should have told her before their first date.

They enjoyed another dining experience and he took her home. He kissed her at her front door and said goodbye. She did not invite him in.

She knew that she was never going to be able to be intimate with him. She knew that was shallow, but she knew herself and she would hyper-focus on his peg leg. They didn't have any further dining experiences.

Chapter 19

CLICKETY-CLACK

CLICKETY-CLACK

They met online and quickly grew to realize that they lived within one mile of one another. They agreed to go to dinner at a local nice restaurant and she agreed to pick him up at his house.

He had a very large custom home in the neighborhood next door and she rang his doorbell. She could hear him clickety clacking on the marble floor all the way to his door. She was curious as to what kind of guy's shoes make a clickety-clack.

He answered and the first thing she did was notice that he was wearing shoes with a lift – essentially high heels. And he was still shorter than her. And she was not that tall herself.

They went to dinner and she found the conversation to drone on. He was boring and not adventurous or athletic. The only positive thing about him was his bank account. Shy of that, she was completely disinterested.

She dropped him off on the way home and they did not have another date.

Chapter 20

PREPARTY ON THE BUS TO U2

PREPARTY ON THE BUS TO U2

He invited her to join a group of his friends on a party bus heading to the Rose Bowl in Pasadena to go to a U2 concert. She agreed and met him at his house and he drove to the meeting point. She met all of his friends and they carried on their merry way,

He brought a cooler on the party bus and they proceeded to drink mixed drinks at a randomly steady pace. By the time they got to the forum, she was well beyond tipsy. Two of the wives were heading to the restroom and they invited her to join.

On her way to the restroom in broad daylight, she peed her pants.

Her jeans were too tight and she was having trouble getting them down and this delay was the cause of the incident.

She smelled like pee the rest of the night and passed out on the bus on the way back. He did not invite her anywhere again.

Chapter 21

SCREENWRITER WATTER

SCREENWRITER WAITER

They met at a bar in Hollywood near where they both worked. They commenced small talk and he was smitten with her. She was a cute Irish gal with bright red hair, freckles, and light blue eyes. She was very funny and witty and charming and also smart. She was a Public Defender in LA and she defended juvenile delinquents.

He was a screenwriter but also a waiter and a high-end restaurant because screenwriting does not pay the rent.

They met several more times at a few local places and he enjoyed her company very much. She was very interesting and full of travel adventures and work crazy stories. She kept him entertained for hours.

The problem was that she found him dull and nonproductive.

He didn't work many shifts as a waiter and had a lot of time on his hands to finish his screenplay that he admitted to working on for the prior decade.

At this rate, he was always going to just be a waiter because his screenplay was never going to be finished.

She stopped seeing him.

Chapter 22

VEGAS OR BUST

VEGAS OR BUST

She was in Vegas for a girls' weekend. He lives there. They meet at a concert at the Sphere and head back to the hotel bar after the concert. They were having drinks and getting to know each other. Her girlfriends had gone to bed after the concert so she was on her own until she needed to get to the airport the next morning. Who needs sleep?

She was a professional businesswoman and owned her own clothing design company in LA. She was interesting and well-traveled and loved live music, culture, art, and travel.

He was a construction defect attorney in Vegas and also enjoyed live music and travel.

They talked into the wee hours of the morning, but it was time for her to catch her flight with her girlfriends back to LA. They exchanged numbers and parted ways.

He agreed to come and visit her in LA the following weekend. He took an Uber from LAX to her house in Brentwood because he didn't want her to get stuck in traffic on a Friday late afternoon.

He stopped for wine and flowers and did not want to show up for their first official date empty-handed. She answered the door and gave him the dime store tour of her two-bedroom condo in the heart of LA. They shared a glass of wine on her patio before walking to dinner.

They enjoyed a nice Italian meal and then went back to her place for a nightcap. They had agreed that if their chemistry matched, he could stay. If it didn't, he would get a hotel nearby.

Chemistry was good on her end but he was so nervous that he could not perform. He had brought ED medicine with him and had taken some earlier but perhaps he took it too early.

She was very understanding about the issue and they had great kissing and cuddling and he was allowed permission to spend the night.

In the morning he took his medicine before she awoke and he went down to get her coffee in bed. He returned with their coffee and proceeded to get frisky again with her. Again, he could not perform. He was mortified.

This had never happened to him. They went out for exercise and returned later in the day. They were planning to shower and head to the beach for a sunset beach walk and dinner. They had a nice time and upon their return to her place, they shared more wine and then cuddled. Again, he could not perform. He was beyond embarrassed.

He left early Sunday morning before she awoke. He left her a note explaining that he was mortally embarrassed and that he couldn't face having it happen to him again.

They did not see each other again.

Chapter 23

64 IS NOT THE NEW 40

64 IS NOT THE NEW 40

He was 46 years old and agreed to meet a lady who claimed to be 40 in Santa Monica for dinner. It was a 3.5-hour drive in traffic for him and a Friday night, He picked her up at her apartment and when she came to his car, he was shocked. She did not look anything like her photos.

She was at least 20 years older than 40 and she weighed double what she disclosed in her photos. She must have weighed 200 pounds. He was mortified.

He honored his commitment to take her for a nice dinner. She ordered two lobsters! He paid the bill and reminded her not to forget her doggy bag.

Chapter 24

TRUMPSTER

TRUMPSTER

They agreed to meet at a local restaurant for dinner. Her pictures look like her as do his. He chose a nice Italian place that they had both enjoyed independently in the past. They agreed to sit at the bar and have dinner there.

They had never discussed politics but apparently, she was hot under the collar to talk about it. Apparently, she was a huge Trump supporter and she believed that if one doesn't support Trump then that person is demented.

Her ex-husband was the most renowned Q-Anon conspiracy theorist and had a widely listened-to podcast. He was also indicted for fraud.

After paying the bill, he politely walked her to her car and that was the end of that.

Chapter 25

DRUNK AND DISORDERLY

DRUNK AND DISORDERLY

They were set up on a blind date by a mutual friend and agreed to meet at the Montage Laguna main bar for a drink. One of his best friends plays the piano there in the evenings and this was the person who set them up.

She was as beautiful as he described and he was handsome with gorgeous blue eyes and silver hair.

She proceeded to get wasted drunk on gin martinis at $25 per drink. She had down four of them in two hours without any food or snacks.

All of a sudden, her personality flipped a switch and she became a mean drunk. She started hitting and kicking him and told him that she didn't want to see him anymore because he wasn't rich enough or handsome enough for her.

Then her personality would flop again and then she would grope him. This went on for about 30 minutes of her flipping and flopping.

He drove her home and asked to use her restroom.

When he went to leave, she was waiting by the front door in her bra and panties. He stepped around her and left.

Chapter 26

GIRL, INTERRUPTED

GIRL, INTERRUPTED

They met at a local bar after a sporting event. She was with her girlfriends and he was with his buddies.

He caught her eye and he bought her a drink. She accepted. They started chatting and discovered that they had a lot in common. For example, they went to the same college but did not know each other. They had friends in common as well.

At the end of the night, they exchanged cell numbers and planned to go out for dinner the following weekend. They meet at a brew pub and have drinks and dinner.

The only problem that she's noting is that she interrupts her constantly. She can't answer a question or tell a story without him interrupting her and talking about himself.

They had a nice night nevertheless and he walked her to her car and gave her a nice kiss goodnight. They had good chemistry and their kiss was juicy.

They agree to meet the following day and go for a hike. Again, she can't get a word in edgewise without an interruption. It is starting to annoy her. After the hike, they agree to grab a drink at a bar nearby. The pattern remains consistent with the interruptions.

She really liked him and they seemed to be very compatible with the exception of his behavior.

She talked with her friends about how much she liked him but that his constant habit of interrupting was annoying.

They agreed that this is not a good habit and one friend suggested that she bring it up with him.

The next they talked she mentioned the issue. He was completely oblivious to his interruptions and promised to pay better attention to them. But it persisted. In fact, it did not improve.

She decided to not pursue the relationship. This habit was not going away and she anticipated that it would get worse. She was disappointed. So was he.

Chapter 27

FOOTY ANYONE

FOOTY ANYONE?

They met on a soccer field for an intramural game post-college. They both played recreational soccer and were on opposite teams playing the same position. She had to guard him and vice versa.

She was an incredible athlete and was very fast on her feet. He could barely keep up with her and she scored on him twice in the first half. His teammates were giving him a hard time saying that he was letting her score in order to hit on her. He did want to ask her out but he was not letting her score on him. She was just fast and accurate. He was impressed and annoyed at the same time.

At the end of the match, after her team won, they all went to a local pub for drinks. He sat next to her and complimented her on her agility, accuracy, and speed. She was competitive and it showed. She told him that she'd been in competitive team sports since childhood.

He had as well but did not have her natural talent. He asked for a date for the weekend and she agreed to have dinner near the college campus.

They met at the restaurant of his choosing and had a great meal together. The conversation flowed with ease. He walked her to her car and gave her a nice kiss. They agreed to go out again soon.

The problem was that her dance card was very full. Between school and work and her athletics, she didn't have as much time available as he did. He also was in school and played soccer for fun, but he did not work.

He was frustrated by the lack of time that she had available for him.

He did not feel like a priority. And to make matters worse, she did not seem to care much. She was noncommittal and unbothered by her business.

Over time, he gave up. She wasn't making time for him but had a dime for the people and things that were her priority.

Chapter 28

1 OBJECT

1 OBJECT

They met for the first time at a deposition in which they were opposing counsel. He was a little cocky and arrogant and she was aggressive. They had immediate mutual attraction and one could cut the sexual tension between them with a dull knife.

The deposition came to a close at the end of the day and he asked her to join him for dinner and drinks near his office. She already had plans for the evening but agreed on a rain check.

She was busy in trial preparations as was he for different cases, so neither was available until the weekend for a dinner date. They agreed on Saturday at a nice restaurant nearby and met for dinner. He was a consummate gentleman and of course, picked out a nice bottle of wine to share and paid the check at the end of the evening before walking her to her car and giving her a kiss goodnight.

He sent her a text message when he got home making sure that she got home okay. She did. They agreed that the following week was too busy with work for them to see one another during the week, but agreed on the following Saturday again.

This pattern went on for a few months and they were enjoying getting to know each other better. But as time wore on the case that they had against each other started heating up. It was a big-money real estate lawsuit and he represented to builder and she represented the owner. She had the stronger case and they spoke of the strengths and weaknesses of both sides on one of their dates. Big mistake.

They should have never talked shop. It was the kiss of death for their relationship. The conversation grew quite heated and they actually got into an argument at the table. People were staring.

They agreed to cut dinner short and see about a reboot for another time. They had crossed the threshold of work during playtime and it seemed irrevocable. They met the next time in court at a mandator settlement conference.

They ultimately settled the case on favorable terms for her client. He had his tail between his legs. They concluded their case together and also their relationship.

Chapter 29

OCTOGENARIAN

OCTOGENARIAN

They both lived in a skilled nursing facility and saw each other daily at meals, bingo, and social activities. They were both in their late 70s and she was a widow and he was a widower. They both had sharp memories still and they were fairly independent. He'd had his hips replaced. She had a new knee. But overall, they were doing well for older people.

One day she garnered the nerve to ask him to join her for dinner. Just the two of them. They often sat near each other for meals or activities, but they had never been solo before.

She dressed in a pretty dress and joined him in the downstairs dining room. He was dressed in a white button-down shirt, sports jacket slacks, and a bow tie. They were adorable together.

They held hands while they talked and he was an attentive listener. He had been a banker in his working years and she had been a receptionist at a dental office.

They carried on dating and enjoying one another's companionship.

Over time though she noticed that he was growing more confused and forgetful. His daughter told her that he had the early stages of dementia and that they all noticed that his memory was slipping quickly.

Within a few months, he didn't recognize her. A few months later, he did not recognize his own family. A few months later he passed away quietly in his sleep surrounded by her and his family.

Chapter 30

RINSE AND REPEAT

RINSE AND REPEAT

They had tried dating one another earlier in the year and it had ended poorly with him standing her up for a dinner date.

He did not have a good excuse other than he was overwhelmed with work and fatherly duties and he just didn't have time to properly date.

Several months passed and his life quieted down and so he reached back out to her to see if she was still single. She was. He was surprised because she was the total package – a catch – but she was picky and particular about her dating prospects because she was a wealthy widow with a good professional career and her adult kids had been launched.

He asked if he could have a second chance at the dinner date and she reluctantly agreed.

She was very upset that he stood her up months prior and was skeptical about giving him another chance. Ultimately, she agreed and this time she was in charge of the choice of the restaurant and the date and the time.

They met at a nice trendy place nearby and he was waiting for her in the bar with a glass of champagne ready for her. He was not going to screw this up twice.

They had a great conversation at the bar which turned into a fun dinner and at the end of the night, he walked her to her car and they had quite the make-out session, He was a great kisser. As was she. Things got a little carried away. She had to slow him down. After all, they were in a crowded parking lot and there were people around and they were both professionals in the area and she did not want anyone she knew to see her getting mauled by this gorgeous stud.

They agreed to meet another time the following weekend and this time after dinner, he invited her to his house for a nightcap. She agreed and they picked up where they had left off in the parking lot.

Things were heating up quickly back at his house and before she knew it, she was naked in his bed with him. They were both sweaty messes and

his room looked like a crime scene with clothes everywhere and an empty bottle of champagne and an open bottle of red wine.

She was not planning on spending the night but that is in fact what happened especially after consuming so much alcohol. She awoke early with the sun and looked over for him. He was already out of bed and she could hear him in the kitchen making coffee. He brought her coffee and breakfast in bed. They enjoyed pillow talk.
As she was sipping her espresso she was startled to see a teenage girl's face poke in. She introduced herself as Lauren who is the 17-year-old daughter of Dad.
She didn't seem shy or surprised to see a naked woman in her dad's bed. This seemed to be the norm.

After the daughter went into the kitchen she observed him put on some more clothes and join his daughter. She sat alone in his bed with the sheets now pulled up. She was going to need to get dressed and do the walk of shame through the kitchen to say goodbye.

It was awkward as she left but what made it most awkward was how normalized it was for the daughter to see her dad in bed with another woman.

He asked her out again the following weekend and they went to another trendy place for dinner. Again, they went back to his place which was closer than her place. She ended up staying again and they had a great time together.

Again, the daughter poked her head into the bedroom the following morning and spoke with her as if she were the mom. Casual and comfortable. It was too casual. Too comfortable.

This scenario went on for months and she wasn't quite sure what she thought of it, but she did like him. He was a very successful businessman and she was a very successful businesswoman. They knew a lot of the same people. They would be considered a power couple if they continued to pursue one another.

The only nagging part was that she felt strange about how comfortable the 17-year-old was with her. Now the daughter sometimes joined them for dinner and he always invited her over after and this was becoming their routine. Things were going well.

She started asking more questions about the daughter and why it was that he had full custody of her. Turns out that Mom was crazy. Certifiable. And a stalker. All not good.

She had some life experience with stalkers and needless to say, never good. Stalkers are bad.

Unbeknownst to her, Mom had been stalking their dates for months. And the sleepovers. She knew way too much and then the unexpected happened.   Mom sent her a friend request on Facebook and Instagram and a connection request on LinkedIn. Things were getting real. She asked Dad about these invitations for a new friend and he told her to delete and block them. She tried, but somehow Mom was able to break through the blocks and deletes and was seriously going to be her bestie whether she wanted to or not.

This went on for weeks to the point where she was constantly looking over her shoulder. She wondered if this wackadoodle was following her to work and to the dates. And it turns out that she was being followed. It was disturbing. She ultimately decided to stop seeing him. She was emotionally invested in both dad and the daughter at this point but she was worried for her safety. This lady was crazy.

Chapter 31

COLLEGE KIDS

COLLEGE KIDS

They met on campus in class. She was a biology major and he was chemistry and they shared the common trait of being Persian. It was clear from the direction of their respective parents that they were expected to date and marry a fellow Persian. The good news was that they were both Persian and smart, handsome, and motivated.

They both were the second child in the Persian two-child family.

The real pressure was on the older sibling so they both shared the more relaxed role of the second Persian success. They dated for years and they were in love.

And then it was time for graduation and that's where the rubber was going to meet the road. She had already applied to law school back East and he was going into education so he was getting his teaching credential in California and his master's degree in education.

She moved to New York. He stayed in the Bay Area. The end.

Chapter 32

COUGARS ROAR

COUGARS ROAR

She met him online on a dating app and he said he was 55. She was in fact 60 so this was not a reach. They met for a date and he looked very young and upon inquiry, he was 25. He was cougar hunting and she was not in the market to be prey. She bought the pacifier sucker a nice meal and they parted ways. She was not a sugar momma.

Chapter 33

SUGAR DADDY

SUGAR DADDY

He held himself out to be a smart successful businessman and she was a hot young thing.

She wanted a rich sugar daddy to pay for her meals and her handbags, outfits, and shoes. He was intrigued.

He took her to dinner at a posh place and he romanced her. That was easy. She was easy. She would sleep with anyone who was willing to pay the bills and pay her attention.

She did sleep with him and he enjoyed this young thing.

But the reality was that he was involved in some bad business dealings in real estate and he had no money but he had plenty of debt.

He was able to squeeze a few more sugar daddy dates out of her before she realized that he was broke.

Chapter 34

ONE MORE COFFEE DATE FOR THE ROAD

ONE MORE COFFEE DATE FOR THE ROAD

She was throwing in the dating towel. Coffee date after coffee date. They all ended the same.

And then she met him. Her last coffee dates. She couldn't believe how gorgeous he was and he was obviously smitten with her. The coffee date went into lunch which went into dinner. They moved in together and are living happily ever after.

Yes, sometimes it works out!

Chapter 35

MILLIONAIRE UNMATCHED

MILLIONAIRE UNMATCHED

One of her girlfriends called and said that she had a guy that she needed to date. She sent the girlfriend pictures and he was handsome and trim. She agreed to allow him to pick her up because they had mutual friends.

He arrived at her place in his Lamborghini SUV which was flashy and loud. He boasted about his wealth the entire night at a five-star hotel restaurant and people were staring at this loudmouth.

She couldn't wait for him to drop her off at home. It was the longest two hours of her life. He was a narcissistic obnoxious man.

When she got home she called her girlfriend and thanked her for thinking of her for the setup and then explained what happened. Her friend was surprised as she had not known this side of him. He was more a friend of her husband's. Millions of dollars can't buy class.

Chapter 36

PLASTIC FANTASTIC

PLASTIC FANTASTIC

They met online and he was fascinated by her sheer beauty. She agreed to meet him for dinner at a nice place nearby. He was there early and dressed well in a pink button-down shirt, jeans, and nice joggers.

She was fashionably late and was wearing a little black dress with heels that showed off her shapely legs. He was impressed by her appearance but a little taken aback by how much makeup she wore and how big her lips were. She looked like every inch of her face had been injected with something. And it also seemed like she altered her photos to look younger and less plastic.

They had a very nice dinner and he enjoyed her company overall, but she seemed very high-maintenance and expensive. He had a decent job but he didn't make enough to support this plastic fantastic. Not to mention the thought of introducing her to his mother and sisters was out of the question.

Chapter 37

GAY BAR RULES

GAY BAR BLUES

He went out one-night solo to a local gay bar for drinks and maybe some dancing with a handsome man. He was dressed to the nines on the Vegas strip and entered the bar with confidence. He was a very handsome, well-kept man.

He immediately noticed a handsome young lad who was saddled up to the bar with a few friends. He seemed very engaged in conversation but didn't seem to be attached to anyone.

He asked the bartender what this young man was drinking and proceeded to send a gin and tonic his way. The young man accepted this gesture picked up his drink and walked over to say thank you.

They proceeded to enjoy conversation and eventually made their way to the dance floor to shake their tail feathers. They were both good dancers and had a very fun experience. At the end of the night, he gave this young man a nice kiss after they exchanged cell information and agreed that they would keep in touch.

He attempted to text and call the young man to no prevail. The guy did not respond to a text message or a text voicemail. It was frustrating as it seemed like they hit it off. Apparently, it was one-sided.

Chapter 38

BIKER BAR

BIKER BAR

She rode her Harley to a local biker bar every Sunday afternoon for a Bloody Mary and a late lunch. She met a group of ladies there often and they knew each other well. Most of her friends were female gay partners and she was one of the few who wasn't seeing anyone.

In walks this petite young thing with short hair and bright blue eyes. She turned everyone's heads. Immediately a Bloody Mary had been ordered and sent in her direction. The cutie approaches and thanks her for the drink and they proceed to sit and chat.

One thing led to another and it wasn't long before Cutie was on the back of the Harley heading to her place. They got it on and it was excellent. The cutie explained that she was actually straight but wanted to see what it was like to be incurious and experiment. Experiment they did. Strap-on – all kinds of fun toys. Cutie had a great time. But she also had a boyfriend.

Chapter 39

MUSIC FESTIVAL

MUSIC FESTIVAL

They met by chance at a music festival in Nashville. She was there with a girlfriend and he was there with a few of his buddies.

He had a hilarious personality and loved country music, dancing, and whooping for no apparent reason. She thought he was hysterical.

She was beautiful and was whooping to get her attention and it worked. They talked a ton the first night and confirmed that they were returning the next

On the second night, they continued to flirt with one another and dance and laugh. They were both having a great time.

She inquired about whether he was going to attend the Saturday night lineup and he told her that he couldn't because he had to pick his girlfriend up at the airport as she was returning from a work trip from France.

Needless to say, she was disappointed that he had a girlfriend and that he was willing to flirt with her despite the girlfriend.

Chapter 40

SUMMER CONCERTS

SUMMER CONCERTS

There are local free summer concerts in the park at various locations near her. She would send out the compilation of concerts to her girlfriends and they would go to quite a few of them. Some venues were on Friday, others on Saturday, and others on Sunday.

She was at a Sunday afternoon concert in the park overlooking the beach with her girlfriends. They went down to the dancing stage and were dancing next to a few guys who didn't appear to be dancing with other women.

One of the guys had particularly lovely eyes and a great smile and he winked at her. She winked back. He danced his way to her and they tried to talk and dance but the music was too loud. He invited her up the hill to where they were sitting so that they could talk.
She followed him.

As they were talking and learning the basics about each other, she asked him about family. He said that he was one of four children and that he had two kids out of wedlock from two different women. That surprised her a lot. He then admitted that he has no relationship with his parents and siblings.

It is at this moment in time that she checked out.

Chapter 41

ROAD TRIP

ROAD TRIP

They met online and had chatted and texted a number of times – the last of which was the night before he was leaving on a road trip from California to Arizona to see his father and then to New Mexico to see other members of the family and ultimately to Denver to see his mom.

As they were chatting, he threw out the idea that she could fly to Denver and road trip home together.

She thought about it for a few hours and then booked a flight to Denver and sent him the confirmation screenshot via text.

He was surprised but delighted as there was no better way to get to know one another than to spend three days solid together.

He picked her up at the Denver airport and he whisked her off to a friend's vacant home in Keystone. They had some wine together and had good conversation, etc. In the morning they set off West back to the San Diego area and they made it near the Utah border. The bigger towns along the way had weekend festivals so they settled on a small town. They checked into a hotel and went out for a hike. After cleaning up, they went to a local pub for dinner. The place was empty but for the owner/bartender named Robin and the cook named Rose.

These two ladies were a hoot and they proceeded to do shots and talk nonstop. The couple was in stitches laughing with these two women. They played some pool and danced and then it was time to go.

They agreed to get up early and try to get as far as they could.

They left before six in the morning and made good time. Before they knew it, they were in St. George, Utah and it was early still.

They were going to stop there, but they agreed that it was only seven hours home and it was too hot to do anything in the desert.

They got to her house took a jacuzzi and had dinner before going to bed. They had a great road trip and he couldn't compliment her enough.

She was beautiful, smart, articulate, and kind and they had so much in common. She thought everything went great as well.

The only thing was that she kept talking about marriage and that she really wanted to marry again. He didn't say anything to her at the time, but the following morning he sent her a text stating that he really liked her but had no interest in getting married again. She responded via text and a telephone call stating that marriage was negotiable, but he did not call her back.

Chapter 42

SNOREFEST

SNOREFEST

They met online and agreed to a dinner date the same day that they started chatting. They were both tired of the dating app Pen pal deal.

She agreed to meet him at a local favorite restaurant and he was seated at the bar when she arrived.

He did not look a thing like his photos. He was overweight, underdressed, and not attractive. She didn't last 15 minutes.

Chapter 43

WHY CANT I RECALL YOUR NAME

WHY CANT I RECALL YOUR NAME

She went out dancing with the girls and it could be said that a guy kept buying her tequila shots and she might have had too much to drink.

He offered to drive her home and stupidly she accepted a ride from this stranger to her home nearby.
She woke up the next morning with some random bloke in her bed and he was clearly a beer (or tequila) goggles late-night bad decision.

And then he had made himself at home, made himself some coffee, and was hanging out on her balcony in her apartment.

She could not remember his name. He finally left because they both had Sunday plans.

The doorbell rang a few hours later and it was a Sunday flower delivery of her favorite flowers. She must have told him in her drunken stoop what she liked.

After the flowers arrived, she went back through her dating app text chains to see if she could remember his name and then she realized that they met at a bar organically and that she had never texted him.

Therefore, it ends with her one-night stand with the guy without a name.

Chapter 45

JUVENILE BREAK-UP TEXT

JUVENILE BREAK-UP TEXT

She met him on a Thursday night for dinner and he asked her to join him at his oceanfront condo for a nightcap. After a bottle of wine for dinner and the nightcap, she could not drive home so he offered her his bedroom. She accepted.

They had a frolic and detour of a night and she barely got any sleep. They both had to work Friday and luckily, she had her work computer with her and was able to work remotely from his place.

She had packed a weekend bag just in case and it turns out that they spent the entire weekend together and it seemed magical.

She left early Monday morning and by the time she got home 45 minutes later, there was a breakup text on her phone.

He loved spending time with her but was not ready for anything serious. She was ready for something serious. She decided that he was a juvenile loser without the courage to call her and talk about his feelings.

She decided to move on. There are lots of adult men who are not juvenile losers in the sea. Time to cast her line again.

LET ME BE THE AUTHOR'S NOTE

Writing poetry is new to me theoretically but in reality, I have been doing it for years when I am upset about something. Therapeutically it is a way to express sadness or frustration.

I wrote Let Me Be for my daughter to explain my feelings regarding loneliness and a desire to find love again. So, I begin this journey of literary magic with poetry dedicated to finding love again.